Walking in Circles

Backpacking the Tahoe Rim Trail

By Jim Rahtz

ISBN-13: 978-1981860043
ISBN-10: 1981860045

Contents

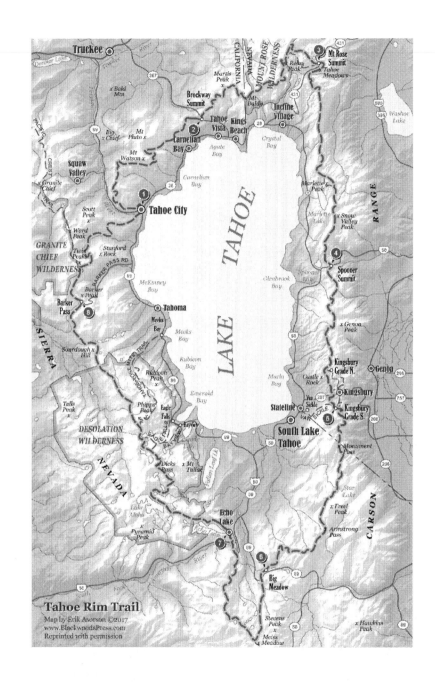

Tahoe Rim Trail

Map by Erik Asorson ©2017
www.BlackwoodsPress.com
Reprinted with permission

"Looks like you're going in circles" is a way to tell someone that they're wasting their time. Talking in circles generally isn't a compliment either. However, walking in a circle can be a good thing for backpackers, provided they're walking around something interesting. Think about it. Logistics become pretty easy. For example, if you leave your car at the start of the trail, it's also waiting for you at the finish! In the case of the Tahoe Rim Trail (TRT), walking in a circle is a great experience.

As you may have guessed from the trail's name, the TRT involves walking around Lake Tahoe, the largest alpine lake in North America. Tahoe is 22 miles long and 12 miles wide, sitting on the border of California and Nevada and nestled between the Sierra Nevada Mountains and the Carson Range. The trail itself is approximately170 miles, so there is more to it than just keeping the lake to your right. In fact, much of the route is in National Forest with other parks and wilderness areas thrown in for good measure. Quite often, the lake itself is out of sight.

The TRT is a great choice for the first-time distance hiker, or anyone that wants a beautiful hike with a minimum of logistical issues to deal with. Beyond not needing a second car or a shuttle, resupplies are also relatively simple. Town stops in South Lake Tahoe and Tahoe City are well spaced and convenient to the trail. If you're flying to the trail, shuttles are established to either town from the Reno, Nevada airport. Summer and early fall feature consistently dry weather. A permit is required for the Desolation Wilderness, but there are no quotas for thru-hikers. Plus, it can be had with a phone call and $20. You'll also need a California Campfire Permit. That one is free for passing an Internet quiz.

In the past, I have always driven to my backpacking destinations. Dealing with getting from the airport to the trail, picking up stove fuel and the like always seemed like more hassle than the drive. However, after driving from Cincinnati to Vermont (twice) for the Long Trail and California for the John Muir Trail, I began to reconsider. The TRT, with its ease of other logistics, seemed like a good one to try, so I looked a little deeper.

Lake Tahoe is a wonder just on its own. It is not only the largest alpine lake on the continent, it's the second deepest lake in America. With its clear blue water, it is just flat beautiful. If the trail just circled the lake, it would be great, but there is much more to it. The trail spends much of its length up away from the lake; even out of sight for significant mileage. The hike is often within National Forest, other parks or in one of three Wilderness Areas.

The loop was going to live up to my expectations with logistics. If flying to the trail, shuttles are regularly scheduled between Reno airport and both Tahoe City and South Lake Tahoe, the two biggest towns on/near the route. As an added plus, the two towns are nearly perfectly opposite from each other on the trail. By starting at one, you can resupply at the other at the halfway point on your hike.

John Muir described the Sierra Nevada as the "gentle wilderness" and the summer weather is typically gentle as well. Generally, the trail is hiked Mid-July through September and the area averages about 2 inches of rain total during that entire period. I walked the trail over ten days in September and there was no rain and maybe 20 minutes of cloud cover during my entire hike. Bring sunscreen. At the elevations on the trail, the temperature is likely to go below freezing during any month of the year. I carried a 23-degree bag and was glad I did.

The trail itself is managed by the Tahoe Rim Trail Association. They have a helpful website and were even more helpful on the phone. The hiking would be considered moderate. You are walking through the Sierras and Carson Range, so there's some considerable up and down. However, unlike the more famous John Muir Trail in the Sierras to the north, the elevation change is less dramatic. Tahoe's shoreline is around 6,300 feet and the high point on the trail tops out at 10,330 feet. The tread is well constructed with switchbacks and even steps on the steeper sections.

The trail is extremely well marked, easy to navigate and rarely confusing. Signage is ample and well located. On the trail I used the Tahoe Rim Trail Pocket Atlas by Blackwoods Press and the TRT phone App by Guthook. Both appeared to be accurate and contained all needed intel.

One of the interesting rules about the TRT is that camping somewhat near the trail isn't discouraged, it's actually required. All camping must be done within 300 feet of the trail corridor. That being said, campers should still attempt to get 100 feet from the trail to camp. That doesn't mean there is a shortage of sites though. The Guthook Guide lists well over 100 spots to set up one or more tents. With that many options, finding a spot to camp was not an issue. On my trip, only once did I set up within sight of another tent; and they were on the opposite side of Dick's Lake.

I found that North Tahoe has a hotel and an "outdoor" store within walking distance of the trail. The hotel, an America's Best Value Inn, was a shuttle stop, wasn't a bad value and would hold a bag of clean clothes for me while I hiked. Sold! I bought my plane ticket for September 7. On past hikes on mountain trails such as the JMT and Colorado Trail, I tended to average about 17 miles per day. Building in a possible zero day at the halfway point would work out to 11 days on the trail. Since this was my first "fly-in" hike, I wanted to include time for flight or trail issues. To be safe, I ended up giving myself up to 13 days to hike before my return flight.

Looking to resupply, I checked out South Lake Tahoe, CA and adjacent Stateline, NV (across the street). Hotels ran the full gamut from a bunkhouse to luxury suites, all within a couple blocks. The Lake Tahoe Resort Hotel was a bit on the expensive side, but was next door to the transit center, contained a laundry and would hold a package for me. Plus, as I found out when I arrived, they had a $2 happy hour. My resupply was set. I just needed to buy my trail food and supplies, as well as get the necessary permits.

My trail food is generally pretty straightforward. Oatmeal or a freeze dried breakfast, a freeze dried dinner and trail mix, prepackaged crackers and bars in between. It might sound pretty boring and it is. Fortunately for me, I was raised without a good cook in the house, so most anything tastes OK. Each day's ration weighed a bit under 1 ½ pounds and I tend to lose weight as I hike.

The permits required are a pretty simple operation to acquire. The California Campfire Permit was free after passing a short Internet quiz. This allowed me to use a camp stove with an open flame. Even with a permit, don't expect to build campfires each night. They are forbidden within the Tahoe Lake Basin. The other needed permit is for camping within the Desolation Wilderness.

There are quotas to get a permit for the Desolation Wilderness, but they do not apply to thru-hikers. Mine was had by calling the Eldorado National Forest Office within two weeks of my arrival date.

When the departure date finally arrived, my pack was checked as baggage and held everything I would need on the trail except a lighter (carry on) and a fuel canister. My carry on was little more than some clean clothes I would leave in Tahoe City to wear after the hike.

After a 2 ½ hour flight to Dallas and another 3 ½ to Reno, the plane began to drop into a dry and brown desert. A drought had been plaguing the area (and most of California) for years. I started to worry that my pack might end up heavier than the low 30s I was planning on. My biggest concern was that, despite my checking with the TRT Association, there would be long stretches with no access to water.

My pack and I arrived in one piece at about 1 pm. I was carrying an almost new Osprey Exos 58. (Osprey replaced my old one under warranty, after it began to deteriorate from 1,500 trail miles.) After an hour or so shuttle I was checked in at the America's Best Value Hotel with the afternoon free to make final preparations and explore.

My first stop was Alpenglow outdoor store, right down the street. There I got a fuel canister, friendly service and a big load of concern. The guy at the counter said he thought the trail was dry for 50 miles past Watson Lake (my first night's stop). Crap! Fifty miles is a helluva long way to carry water. That much weight in my pack could be a backbreaker for me. (In case you're wondering, very little of the TRT is actually within easy walking distance of Lake Tahoe. It's not like I would be able to dip a cup in the lake whenever I got thirsty.)

I made a phone call to the Tahoe Rim Trail Association and they confirmed that their website was correct; the trail was dry, but not that dry. There would be water where I was planning on it. I would have to venture off the trail at times, but my longest dry spell would be under 20 miles. Whew. It was definitely time to head to the Tahoe Mountain Brewing Company to settle my nerves and have a late lunch.

Not being a huge fan of heavy, craft beers, I asked the barmaid what they had that was close to Bud Light. Her reply was, "We have water," but she gave me a sample of a brew that worked. The TRT website warned that sweat bees were thick around the northern part of the trail. I wasn't concerned about that until I got stung in the back while sitting at the bar.

I spent the rest of the day checking out the beautiful lake, walking to the trail (1/2 mile) and repacking the pack. Dropping off a small case of clean clothes at the front desk and hitting the Blue Agave next door for a filling Mexican dinner completed all my tasks. There was nothing left to do but wait until morning and start walking.

Décor at the Blue Agave

"Another glorious day, the air as delicious to the lungs as nectar to the tongue."
John Muir, My First Summer in the Sierra

Being used to Eastern Daylight time, it was difficult to stay in bed until 6, but I managed. After taking my last shower for the next 5 or 6 days I wandered down to the hotel's free continental breakfast. There was coffee and OJ, but all the food options were prepackaged buns and doughnuts. Actually, it was a perfect way to prep my system for all the processed and freeze-dried food I'd be eating over the next 170 miles; so, I was good.

After rechecking everything one last time, I began walking the half mile through Tahoe City to the trail. My pack was heavy with 3 liters of water. While I started right next to the lake, I wouldn't be near it for long. Once I hit the trail, I began my clockwise circle with a moderate but long upgrade, leaving the lake and its 6,225 foot elevation behind. Despite the cool (39 degree) morning, I was down to a t-shirt and shorts almost immediately. As always when I start a long hike, I was in great spirits; full of anticipation.

Climbing through the pine forest there was the pleasant call of some assorted birds, but also an ongoing drone. Not a flying around, missile packing drone, but the noise. Sweat bees were everywhere. None of them stung, but every time I stopped, especially if I was in the sun, they would swarm around me.

As I climbed, I started getting better and better views of gorgeous Lake Tahoe, though it was a bit hazy looking into the morning sun. Away from the lake were some nice views toward the surrounding mountains. When I stopped for a snack at a pretty overlook, the bees moved in; so I made it quick.

After an hour or so I covered myself in sunscreen as there wasn't a cloud to be seen and the forest was fairly open. There was no need to treat my lower legs as they already had a protective layer of dust from the dry trail.

Through the morning I passed several mountain bikers and a couple day hikers. The path was easy to follow and any intersections were marked well enough. Only one backpacker crossed my path and he was going the other way, seemingly on a mission. He barely raised his head long enough to say hey.

With the climb and photo breaks, I was averaging about 1 ½ miles per hour. At that pace I figured to make Watson Lake and the first water by about 4 pm. It was 13 ½ miles in, so it seemed like that would make a good first day. At five miles, the trail hit 7,600 feet and then bounced between 7,200 and 7,800 for the rest of the day. At around mile 10, the trail began to follow what was once a road. It had grown back, but was relatively flat and straight. The sky remained clear and the air was warm, but not hot. Despite a bit of heal pain, I made good time through the afternoon. The sweat bees encouraged me to keep moving as well.

It was only around 3 pm when I arrived at Watson Lake with a half-liter of water to spare. It seemed early to stop for the day, plus there was a road to the lake and I figured I'd end up with company. Only hours into the hike, I wasn't yet craving the sound of a human voice. So, I filtered a couple liters of water, loaded up with 2 more and kept walking. It would be seventeen miles to the next water.

In another half mile I spotted a nice spot just right for one tent. Shaded by some big pines, there were relatively few bees. With the pack weighed down with 4 liters of water, it was an easy decision to call it a day. The tent was quickly up and I laid inside for a bit until hunger called me back out. Mountain House Beef Stew; a meal I take on nearly every backpacking trip. I'm not a picky eater and the reconstituted casserole hit the spot. A breeze kept the bugs at bay until sundown when the quickly dropping air temperature also assisted in that regard.

Some of the information I had researched before leaving spoke of bear canisters being a good idea. Since I had one from hiking the JMT, I went ahead and brought it. It adds about two pounds to the pack, but it saves time each evening searching for the right branch to hang the food. Plus, the open coniferous forest didn't provide a multitude of good "bear trees." The "Bearikade" canister was chock full, but with a little persuasion, everything fit. I stuck the canister into the triple fork of a nearby tree.

Once the sun was completely down, a half-moon began shining bright through the pines. The temperature dropped significantly, and I was wearing my fleece and down vest by the time I hit the bag around 8:30. Despite it being my first night of the hike, the peacefulness of the surroundings lulled me quickly to sleep.

Morning arrived clear and cool and the first few downhill miles went fast. I was getting back down near the lake level and the forest became relatively thick. Once at the Brockway Trailhead though, things began to change. At an altitude of 7,000 feet the drop reversed into a long climb. After a couple miles of climbing, I arrived at View Point and a gorgeous overlook of the lake. It was near there that I met Lydia and her dog. They were thru-hiking in the other direction. She was on day seven, having started at Big Meadow. I let her know the water situation ahead and wished her luck. At our current paces, I thought I might see her again on the other side of the lake, but never did.

View from near View Point

The trail continued to climb and after approximately 13 miles for the day I arrived at Mt Rose Wilderness. The area was named after the nearby 10,785-foot extinct volcano. Through there things were wide open for miles and I began to bake in the sun while continuing to climb. The four liters of water from the day before were all but gone. Another couple miles got me to the Grey Lake cutoff. By this point I had climbed to well over 9,000 feet. It was over a half mile downhill to Grey Lake. I didn't want to give up my hard earned altitude, but it was the only sure water in the area. I arrived to find a beautiful creek with cold water flowing into the small scenic lake. My timing was perfect as, by then, my water bottles were empty.

I thought about moving on, but it was 4 pm and the climb back out would have been rough at the end of the day. Plus, I would have had to carry extra water out to dry camp. After arguing with myself for a bit, I finally decided to park it. The creek water was so cold it hurt my feet as I cleared the dust off them. Very tasty too. (The water, not my feet.)

There were several nice spots to camp around the lake. A couple more hikers showed up around 6 pm. They had one more day to complete their thru-hike and picked a site out of sight and sound from mine. It turned out to be a nice quiet evening around the lake.

Rocky climb from Grey Lake

The night at Grey Lake was a bit warmer than the night before, probably in the mid-forties. For the second night, I slept with my water filter. The first night was to keep it from freezing. Apparently the second night was just so it didn't feel unwanted. Despite that awkwardness, I slept pretty well and got rolling on Day 3 by around 7:15. (For water filtration, I used a Sawyer Squeeze Mini. It only weighs about 2 ounces and does a great job of making the water safe to drink. A weakness of this, and some other filters, is that letting them freeze will destroy the filter medium. At that point, rather than a water filter, they become little more than a Giardia pipeline. Don't let your filter freeze.)

In a move that will certainly upset any purists, I climbed out of the Grey Lake camp on a different trail than I came in on. This put me back on the TRT a bit beyond where I had left it; near what was left of Mud Lake. I suppose I could have stayed on the TRT and got my water at Mud Lake, but as it looked more like Mud Puddle, I was happy that I had made the detour. Regardless, the climb out was significant and rocky, making me doubly glad that I didn't try it the evening before, laden with water.

Once back on the TRT, the path kept climbing. There was nothing extreme, but several miles with long switchbacks and even a few stairs. While I rarely use my music collection on the trail, I have been known to sing to myself on a tough climb. Generally, I end up with a single song playing over and over in my head for the whole trail. On the TRT, the obvious choice was "Roundabout," released by the English rock group Yes in 1971. This could be the official tune of the trail. Not only did the title match the route, but the lyrics did too.

I completed the climb to the top of Relay Peak at about 9:30. I was at 10,330 feet and the highest point on the trail. Nearby was a great spot to take in the views and relax with a snack. For whatever reason, the bees weren't hanging around at that altitude.

Looking south at the Carson Range

Heading down the back side of Relay Peak, I soon had the option of 5 ½ miles of new trail or 4 ½ miles of old trail/road. Not wanting to offend purist hikers even more, I took the longer trail even though that meant some additional climbing. On the plus side, the new route was well built. As it was Saturday and the weather was perfect, I started meeting a significant number of day hikers. One stuck in my mind as he was wearing a shirt I'd never seen before. On it were photos of famous Native American warriors. Wording was "Homeland Security: Fighting Terrorism Since 1492." I guess everything is a matter of perspective.

The night at Grey Lake was a bit warmer than the night before, probably in the mid-forties. For the second night, I slept with my water filter. The first night was to keep it from freezing. Apparently the second night was just so it didn't feel unwanted. Despite that awkwardness, I slept pretty well and got rolling on Day 3 by around 7:15. (For water filtration, I used a Sawyer Squeeze Mini. It only weighs about 2 ounces and does a great job of making the water safe to drink. A weakness of this, and some other filters, is that letting them freeze will destroy the filter medium. At that point, rather than a water filter, they become little more than a Giardia pipeline. Don't let your filter freeze.)

In a move that will certainly upset any purists, I climbed out of the Grey Lake camp on a different trail than I came in on. This put me back on the TRT a bit beyond where I had left it; near what was left of Mud Lake. I suppose I could have stayed on the TRT and got my water at Mud Lake, but as it looked more like Mud Puddle, I was happy that I had made the detour. Regardless, the climb out was significant and rocky, making me doubly glad that I didn't try it the evening before, laden with water.

Once back on the TRT, the path kept climbing. There was nothing extreme, but several miles with long switchbacks and even a few stairs. While I rarely use my music collection on the trail, I have been known to sing to myself on a tough climb. Generally, I end up with a single song playing over and over in my head for the whole trail. On the TRT, the obvious choice was "Roundabout," released by the English rock group Yes in 1971. This could be the official tune of the trail. Not only did the title match the route, but the lyrics did too.

for Tuesday (three days away). I'd have to wait and see on that one.

Several people walked by carrying large canisters of grizzly spray, which seemed like tremendous overkill as there are no grizzlies in either California or Nevada. One of the bearophobes was also a self-appointed trail safety manager. He began quizzing me to make sure I'd survive the upcoming cool night. I told him I'd be happy down to 25 degrees, miserable below 15 and only risk becoming a frosty corpse if the temperature dropped below zero. (The forecast was for 35.) A few mountain bikers were wearing bear bells as well. Between the bells one guy was wearing and his girlfriend loudly making fun of him about it as they rode, I knew they would be 100% safe; from bears anyway.

(By the way, the website of the North American Bear Center, bear.org, also states that grizzly spray is overkill for black bears. Their research showed that weaker concentrations of spray, designed for dogs, worked consistently to stop approaching black bears.)

After passing on a few large open campsite opportunities, I spotted a pretty little spot within some tall pines, but with a bit of a view. I was done for the day around four. One of my favorite freeze-dried meals, pasta primavera, was on the menu.

After dinner I walked about 200 yards back up the trail to a tremendous lake overlook near the 46 ½ mile mark of the trail. The spot came complete with a comfortable rock chair to sit and watch the sunset. It was a great way to end the day. I was able to snap some photos and used one of them for the cover of this book. While the area was crowded during the day, it appeared that I was the only person spending the night. It was a relatively warm night (in the 40s) with a great star show.

After a quick stroll back to the overlook to watch the sunrise, I packed up and began hiking by 7. I made pretty good time early on and began seeing runners heading the other way. All were moving fairly slowly. Sharing a break with one, it turned out they were participants in a 204 mile race around Lake Tahoe. They had started a couple days earlier with a time limit of 100 hours. I saw maybe 30 runners that had completed 120-130 miles to that point. A few of them were smiling and talking. Most were grim. In fact, a couple looked like they were barely staying ahead of the grim reaper.

I've run many trail races. I've even run a few marathons, but I couldn't even comprehend wanting to race 200+ miles. I didn't even know how to cheer them on. "Looking good! Only 80 miles to go?"

The trail was flat to downhill and the walking continued to be easy. It was a good thing as I needed to make significant miles on that day. By mid-morning I was in Lake Tahoe (Nevada) State Park and there were only 2 areas where I could legally camp. Marlette Camp was right on the trail, but I reached there by early afternoon; too early to stop. North Canyon Camp was five miles further down the trail, but required hiking a mile and a half down a side trail. I decided to hike all the way out of the park before stopping. I did stop at Marlette Campground for a snack and to refill my water supply. The well water was my first option since Ophir Creek, 13 miles back. The well was potable, though a sign said it was tad high in aluminum. Since I lose the opportunity to drink beer out of aluminum cans while on the trail, a little extra in the water was probably fine; keeping my metal levels stable.

From there the trail started climbing, eventually getting back to 9,000 feet. The stretch was on a high ridge running the east side of that lake. It bounced on either side of ridge top for a bit giving views of both the lake and mountains to the east. (In and out the valley.) I eventually spent several miles overlooking the lake with great views of Tahoe and Marlette Lakes. Unfortunately, the wide-open vistas meant few trees, no shade and howling wind. It was to the point that I had trouble keeping my hat on. I just wanted to get that stretch over with.

Looking over Marlette Lake to Lake Tahoe

As I began to drop away from the views, I needed water for the night and morning and there wasn't any on the trail for a while, so I cut off toward Spooner Lake. The guide showed restrooms and water on far side of the lake if I didn't want to filter the turbid lake water. I didn't. It had been a long day and the 1 ½ mile detour went slowly. I tried the first cutoff hoping water was there, but it was just an empty parking lot. I kept walking for a while among a number of day hikers. Finally, I ask a gentleman walking the trail if he knew where the restrooms and water were. He said he saw some portalets, but the restroom was under construction. My heart just sank, but I kept walking. Eventually I spotted the under-construction restrooms, but outside the construction zone was a hydrant. Yeah! I'd have been up a creek without that water.

Near the hydrant were a couple guys sitting under a pop up booth. Turns out they were support for a bike race, had burritos in a warmer and offered me some. That detour was getting better all the time. I ate my unexpected Trail Magic dinner, loaded up with 4 liters of water and headed back down the trail. I even crossed paths with a couple deer as I walked back along Spooner Lake. The burritos gave me energy to climb the steep hill at the park's exit and I continued to the first decent camp spot I could find. With the water detour, I had walked around 21 miles and was beat.

It stayed windy throughout the night, rattling the tent and making sleep difficult. I was up before first light, had a granola bar for breakfast and was moving by 6:40. I was looking at a four-mile climb to Lake View then 12 or so more miles to my resupply in South Lake Tahoe.

The climb was significant, but not overly difficult and in approximately two hours I topped out to a really cool view of the lake. Standing at near 9,000 feet, with the temp around 40 and the wind howling, it wasn't just cool, but downright cold. I took some quick pictures and moved on. Once off the edge of the rim, the updraft wind eased off quite a bit.

The next nine miles were mostly downhill, dropping close to 2,000 feet in the stretch. With visions of a hot shower and cold beer I was hustling and made it to Kingsbury Grade by noon. There's a road (Route 207) crossing there and the local bus service uses it. You'd be tempted to jump onto the road and hike it towards town and the closest bus stop. Don't. The road is winding, steep, not safe to walk along and the bus stop is nowhere close. Continue on the trail another few miles and take a half mile side trail right to a bus stop at Stagecoach Lodge. Eighty one miles down, 89 to go.

View near Kingsbury Grade

The $2 fare delivered me to the Stateline Transit Center which happened to be next door to the Lake Tahoe Resort Hotel. The place was very nice; maybe too nice for a hiker, but I wasn't complaining. I had picked it after a short Internet search because it was next to the bus stop, had a laundry on site, accepted a mailed resupply package and had a room available. At $120 per night, it was more than other lodging in the area, but also much fancier. My "suite" had a separate living area, three TVs and a truly spectacular shower. My opinion of the shower may have been affected by it being my first shower in nearly a week though. On top of that, the daily happy hour not only had $2 beer, but also free snacks. It looked like my evening was set.

Checking the TV weather forecast in the morning, there was indeed rain approaching. The day (Tuesday) was looking like it could be a wash out. Since I had plenty of time to finish the trail before my flight back, I made the less than difficult decision to stay in the lap of luxury another night. Unfortunately, when I tried to book a 2nd night, they stated they were full. It was back to the web where I found a room a block away. I'd be moving to the Alpine Inn. It was slightly lower on the indulgence scale, but at $55/night, the cost matched the opulence. My room was clean, so it was fine.

Beyond switching hotels and strolling a quarter mile to Sports LTD for a fresh fuel canister, the "day off" was chore free. The rain fizzled out by mid-morning so the cool cloudy day would have been perfect for hiking. It was also perfect for relaxing and my legs weren't protesting about the lack of work. I visited the lakefront, the Explore Tahoe Visitor Center, a couple great restaurants and, of course, revisited the $2 Happy Hour. In addition, just across the street was

Nevada and a couple casinos. Since I feel that backpacking solo is enough of a gamble, I steered clear of those.

My second morning in South Lake Tahoe found me eager to be back on the trail. I caught the first bus (7:20 AM) heading back to the trail and by 8 I was off the bus, done with the side trail and back on the TRT. The bear canister was full, but with more water available on this half of the trail, I was only carrying two liters and felt light on my feet.

Despite being at the southwest corner of the lake, the trail continued heading in a generally southern direction for the next 25 miles, getting well away from regular views of the trail's namesake. The path climbed into taller mountains that still harbored significant snow near their peaks. The big granite boulders were reminiscent of hiking near Yosemite. Lunch was by Star Lake, a beautiful snow fed spot where I refilled my water before continuing the climb.

The grade was moderate, but unrelenting until I made it to Freel Pass. At 9,700 feet there were some tremendous views. Along the way I passed a couple pushing their bikes/camping equipment up the trail. The woman talked to me about how hard it was to push her load up the hill. It didn't look fun. At a certain point the bike just became a poorly designed wheelbarrow. Of course, when they flew by on the next downgrade she was not complaining.

Dropping from Freel Pass, the trail is etched into a pretty steep mountainside. As I stepped aside (as much as possible) to let a few mountain bikers by, one told me, "Thank you so much! I'm scared to death of heights!" It never ceases to amaze me how often I meet people scared of heights while I'm "in heights." She was not enjoying her chosen recreation.

With about 16 miles in for the day, I was hiking the high, wide ridge of Freel Meadow. There were great views of either the distant Lake Tahoe to the north or impressive mountains to the south. It seemed like a good time to stop for the night and I picked a spot with a stunning, southern view. With the tent sitting exposed at about 9,200 feet, it looked like I would be in for a cold night. I ended up sleeping with the water filter again to make sure it didn't freeze.

Freel Meadow Campsite

Despite being warm and comfortable, I rolled out of the sleeping bag at about 6. The morning was indeed cold and windy. The chill made it tough to put away the tent, plus the ground cover was mysteriously wet. (I am getting old, but my prostate hasn't failed me yet.) Breakfast was cold as I wasn't sure I could get water to boil. That saved a little time so I was packed up and rolling by 7. Unfortunately, as I started hiking, I became somewhat dizzy. Not a good sign. This has happened on other long trips and I hadn't figured out what the cause was for sure. The plan for the day was to stay hydrated and try to camp at a lower altitude. (After the trip, I got checked out and found it was most likely a combination of dehydration and sleeping without a pillow that affected my inner ears.)

The trail continued heading away from Lake Tahoe, the day warmed nicely and the scenery became even more impressive. Much of the day was spent traveling through multiple big meadows, such as aptly named Big Meadow, surrounded by rugged mountains. At one point, my leg became mysteriously wet and I finally realized the issue. One of my water bottles had cracked. (Frozen the night before?) With the western side of the trail having more access to water, it was not the huge problem it could have been.

Despite the topography I was making great time, getting to Round Lake for lunch and Showers Lake by 2 pm. The spot was so lovely, I almost called it a day, but decided to press on. By this time the trail had turned north again.

Water would get a little scarce for a while so I committed to a campsite/water stop listed in the guide that was around six miles past Showers Lake. It was a tough climb, but the rugged beauty kept me going. The trail ran along with the Pacific Crest Trail (PCT) in this area and I spent a little time chatting with a southbound thru-hiker. He confirmed the stream was still flowing near my chosen site for the night and I convinced him to make Showers Lake his destination.

Showers Lake

As I continued on, there were more discussions with other southbound PCT backpackers. They were all very nice and all very young. At 58, I still hadn't gotten used to being called sir.

Eventually the trail was back to where there was an occasional glimpse of the lake. I rolled into my chosen site at about 5 pm for a 20 ½ mile day. The stream was but a trickle, but enough. The altitude was 8,400 feet and I drank throughout the day, so I was hopeful there'd be no dizziness in the morning. I had plenty of time for an Alpine Air freeze-dried orange pineapple chicken entree. It did not live up to my high hopes in the taste realm.

Dizziness free, Day 8 began by dropping down a steep hill then passing thru another ski resort. The trail actually passes through several resorts as it travels around the lake. After crossing a main road (Rt 50) near mile 122 I arrived at what was described in my guide as a seasonal stream. I expected at most a trickle, but this was a raging torrent. Much smaller streams than this have been bridged, but it was time to break out the wading sandals. Two guys heading the other way had tried to throw their packs across and it went badly, costing them their GPS. I took a test trip to make sure I could handle it, then went back and re-crossed with my pack. On the plus side my feet got power washed.

After the rough creek crossing the trail and I climbed for a while. I had an interesting conversation with Gray Cricket (trail name; not an actual cricket) who was section hiking the PCT up to Mt Larson. Sitting for a snack break I was interrupted by a chipmunk (animal; not a trail name) trying to get into my pack. This was a popular stretch of trail and they'd learned.

The next point of interest was Echo Lake. The reservoir is man-made and generates electricity, which was probably why the creek was high. Stunning vacation homes surround it and are only reachable by foot or boat. The store at Echo Lake is also a great place for snacks and a milkshake, provided you get there before Labor Day. In mid-September, all I could do was longingly stare through locked windows. There was a parking lot with plenty of day hikers and some backpackers that were heading, with me, toward the Desolation Wilderness and Lake Aloha.

The trail ran behind several vacation homes before the steep, rocky climb out away from Echo Lake into Desolation Wilderness. Most of the day hikers seemed to have turned back by this point. The trail was pretty open and, as always on this hike, sunny. Near Lake Aloha there was a trail intersection that was a bit confusing. I checked my GPS and it told me I was a half mile off the TRT. Everything seemed fine on the map, but without the GPS to agree, I began to lose confidence. Thankfully, while sitting under a tree rereading the map, two hikers showed up and assured me I was right and the GPS was wrong.

Lake Aloha

Once I got to Lake Aloha, it was clear why the area was called Desolation Wilderness. The landscape was extraordinarily stark, with few trees and bare rock (boulders and cliffs) all around the lake. Some snow was still hanging on above the lake in the September sun. Aloha is a popular place to camp; interesting, but too desolate looking for me. I moved on.

As mentioned earlier, there is a permit required to camp within the Desolation Wilderness, and there are quotas in place to protect the area from overuse. Thru-hikers also need a permit, but are not affected by the quota. The only issue is that you cannot apply for the thru-hiker permit until two weeks before you enter the wilderness. Seems like no big deal until you figure the fact that I'd already been walking for over a week, had a day of travel time, and they mail you the permit. I had received mine the day before I left for the hike.

Continuing my walk, I arrived at Susie Lake about 2:30. It was absolutely beautiful, had nice spots to pitch a tent and the trail to it had been rocky and rough. By all accounts I should have stopped for the day. I was far enough that I could finish in 2 days and the next good camp spot was a difficult six miles away.

Unfortunately, when I'm by myself, that simple logic doesn't work. I can be at a spot so picturesque that you get a lump in your throat, but without someone there to share it with, after a couple minutes it just seems sad and lonely. These times make me consider whether to keep doing long solo hikes. Sharing the moment with a text or email might have helped, but since I had a certain wireless carrier, I'd never know for sure. On every hike, I find extensive mileage where other carriers provide service and mine does not. That one percent difference seems to be centered over every trail I hike.

So, I decided to move on over Dicks Pass to Dicks Lake, 6 miles and a 1,600 foot climb and 1,000 foot drop away. The climb was open to the sun, rocky and unrelenting. In an effort to ease the weight of the load I only brought one liter of water, and that quickly proved to be less than enough. After only a mile or so, the plan was looking like a mistake. I was tired, hot and already dehydrated.

Normally I frown on it in the wilderness, but music can help people through a tough effort. I pulled out my earphones and set the phone's playlist to shuffle. The impact was instant. I could feel my heart rate rise and my pace quicken.

A couple fast tunes had me moving right along. "Too Old to Die Young" (Brother Dege) had me thinking I might be pushing too hard. Then "L'estasi dell'oro {The Ecstasy of Gold} (Ennio Morrricone) came on. If you're unfamiliar with it, it's from the classic Western, The Good, the Bad and the Ugly: the cemetery scene. If you haven't seen it in a while, go to YouTube and watch the scene. I'll wait……

By the time that song was over I was practically jogging up the mountain. The only thing to slow me down was hearing one of the songs from the U2 album that was automatically downloaded to every iTunes account. I really have to find out how I can delete that.

Looking toward Half Moon Lake from near Dick's Pass

After a while I came across a PCT hiker filling up at a small spring. As I grabbed a little water too, he told me I was very close to the top. Again, things are often all about perspective. For someone that just walked there from Canada, it probably did seem close. After another 20 minutes I was still climbing. It was definitely a struggle to get there but view at the top was terrific in both directions. On a break near the crest I enjoyed the superb view in the company of a couple marmots.

Despite being tired and still thirsty, I can always go downhill. Well-built switchbacks dropped down the north slope which appeared to be great habitat for the rugged hemlock tree. I kept moving and made it to Dick's Lake by 5:30. Lightheaded, but there. Another 20+ mile day. A few other groups were camping, but there were plenty of spots around the lake and I quickly had my tent nestled in the pines on a bed of soft needles.

As soon as I settled in, the coyotes started. I'm not sure how long the yipping serenade lasted as I was quickly fast asleep. The day put me 137 miles into the 170 mile trip.

I once again got an early start in the morning, walking by just after 7. Several groups were camping around the lake, but I was first one moving. The trail stayed open and rocky as I dropped by more beautiful lakes and campsites. My morning snack was a Larabar apple pie bar. I'm not quite sure why it got that name. From my perspective, if you don't expect it to taste like Mom's, or Mrs. Smith's, or any apple pie you've ever had, it's not bad.

Eventually, as I dropped, the trail returned to the forest and the tread smoothed out. Once again, it was another magnificent day as I strolled downhill for miles. Just before Richardson Lake, I got my first glimpse of Lake Tahoe in a while, but it soon disappeared. All good things, like the downhill, come to an end and I was looking at another climb. It was nothing like the previous day's though. Heading north, with the sun at my back, the climb wasn't too bad even though I was carrying more water in an ongoing attempt to avoid being overly dehydrated.

Near the end of the climb was Barker Pass Trailhead and good numbers of day hikers. I talked with several folks and was followed for a bit by someone's drone (the flying, irritating kind). Based on the blinking red light, the high-pitched noise machine seemed to be signaling to me. In an international language I thought it might understand, I signaled back. It apparently took the hint and flew off to disturb somebody else's outdoor experience.

Once I finally got close to topping out there were some great views of the big lake. After a short break to take in the sight, I dropped back down a bit and found a campsite near a small stream. The site was small and dusty, but I was tired and needed water. It would do after another 20 mile day. Tahoe City was nearly in reach!

After dinner, about 7 pm, I climbed into the tent to relax and read for a few minutes. Next thing I knew, it was about 5:30 the next morning. After 10+ hours of sleep it seemed like a good time to get moving. I packed up by headlamp and started down the trail just as it began to get light.

The trail dropped a little way while being etched into the side of some rugged cliffs. I was around 8,000 feet and starting to see the beginnings of fall color developing around me. It wasn't long before the drop ended and the path began the climb up towards impressive Twin Peaks. After several switchbacks I entered Granite Chief Wilderness; no permit required. A few groups were camping there and I assumed the crowd must be due to it being the weekend. Just below the peaks the PCT split off and I turned for Tahoe City.

Fall color starting near Twin Peaks

After a couple more views of the lake the trail began a long drop into the woods. Over the miles the trail smoothed out and leveled out, eventually turning into an old forest service road. I knew I was getting close to civilization as I started meeting walkers with dogs. You can tell how far you are from a parking lot based on the size of the dog. Once you see a Dachshund or a Bichon, you're within a half mile.

I was speaking with a woman with three Belgian Shepherds (2-3 miles from a parking lot). She asked, "Where you from? You got an ache-sent!"

"Cincinnati, and from where I'm standing, you're the one with the accent." (All about perspective.)

With that, she couldn't stop laughing. "Har har. Ache-sent!" She ended up telling me about a couple restaurants to try.

Right on cue, based on my dog mileage meter, I came to a parking lot. The trail continued across the street, hit another forest service road and went straight up the hill, possibly the steepest half mile of the entire trail. This was not over yet.

Knowing I had to be getting close, I kept pushing as the trail flattened out. I passed through a grove of yellowing aspen, across a meadow and finally to a sign saying Tahoe City: 2 miles.

The path dropped for most of two miles to a park, joined a bike/hike trail and crossed a bridge over the nearly empty Truckee River. Across the street was the hill I started up to begin the journey. I'd hiked either 170 or 173 miles depending on which guide I looked at. Regardless, it was just after noon and I was done! I'd hiked the last 75 miles in 3 1/2 days. I don't recommend that pace. Regardless, it was a great hike. Challenging, but very doable with new mountain beauty unveiling itself with every turn of the trail.

On the half mile walk up to the hotel, I swung into a grocery store for a Coke and a razor. A two-week neck beard looks good on no one. Once showered up and in my clean, non-hiking clothes, I hit the Blue Agave Mexican restaurant again. It seemed a little ironic as I had carried tortillas for the whole trip and never touched one. I had planned on hiker hunger to kick in and, on this hike, it never did.

With a day before my flight back, I got the shuttle to the Reno Airport and rented a car. To kill time I visited their great automobile museum and later found a trail to take a hike. Of course, it was a loop trail.

Near Dick's Pass

As I said, the logistics for this trail were easier than most, but there are always preparations to complete. There are certainly other options, but below is how I went about things.

Initial Research and Guides: The first place to start your research is the TRT website, https://tahoerimtrail.org/
Guthook has a phone App which provides a trail map, elevations, water and campsite locations.
The Blackwoods Press Guide provides much of the same information without being dependent upon your phone's battery. http://blackwoodspress.com/
Transportation: From the Reno Airport to Tahoe City I used the North Lake Tahoe Express http://www.northlaketahoeexpress.com/.
A similar service can get you to South Lake Tahoe http://southtahoeairporter.com/
The bus to and from the TRT at South Lake Tahoe was Route 23 of the Tahoe Transportation District.
http://www.tahoetransportation.org/images/assets/transit/201 6_map_schedules/Riders_Guide_2016_Rte_23.pdf

Resupply: The Lake Tahoe Resort Hotel accepted packages for guests so I mailed most of my resupply needs to them. As I planned for five days for each half of the trail, I mailed myself four breakfasts and five days' worth of lunches, dinners and snacks. In addition, the package contained a travel-sized toothpaste, hand sanitizer, sunblock and contact lens solution. I also included a single use detergent "pod" and a dryer sheet. To eliminate the need for either two loads or to wear rain pants while doing laundry, I filled out the package with an old t-shirt and shorts.

The only resupply item I purchased in South Lake Tahoe was a fuel canister at the nearby Sports LTD.

Hotels: In Tahoe City I stayed at America's Best Value Inn. The room was clean and comfortable. Pluses were its proximity to the trail, it served as a stop on the airport shuttle route, held clothes for my return, was located close to a laundry and actually was a good value.

In South Lake Tahoe I stayed at the Lake Tahoe Resort Hotel. The room was extremely nice. Pluses were its proximity to the Transit Center, an onsite laundry and they hold (resupply) packages. I also stayed at the Alpine Inn. The room was dated, but clean and comfortable. Pluses were proximity to the Transit Center and they were the first hotel I contacted that had a room available.

Permits: Despite campfires being prohibited on the trail, a California Campfire Permit is required if you plan on using a stove. It can be had for free by visiting preventwildfireca.org and passing the online quiz.

A permit is required to camp in the Desolation Wilderness. Typically, there is a quota for the permits, but thru-hikers can bypass the quota by calling the Eldorado Forest Service office at (530) 543-2694 within two weeks of your intended camping dates. The cost in 2017 was $20.

Bears: Bearproofing of all food and "smellables" is required on the TRT. The simplest and most successful method is to use a bear canister.

While I don't proclaim to be a backpacking gear expert, I did spend quite a bit of time researching, testing and living with the gear I used on the trail. It may have been just luck, but all my equipment worked, for the most part, flawlessly. Most of the gear listed below was used not only on the TRT but also on thru-hikes of the Colorado Trail, Long Trail and John Muir Trail. That's a total of about 1,200 miles in pretty varied conditions. Not counting food, water and the bear canister, my pack weight ran around 20 pounds.

Pack – Osprey Exos 58, size large. The pack weighs only 2 lb, 12 ounce and has a 61 liter volume. It was comfortable handling a 25-30 pound load, but has carried close to 40 lb. when necessary.

Tent – Big Agnes Copper Spur UL 1 which only tips the scale at 2 lb, 3 ounce, is self-standing and was big enough that, at 6 foot, 3 inches, I didn't feel overly cramped. It set up quick and on other trips has held up to some significant storms. Ventilation could be better, but it isn't bad. For another 4.5 ounces I got the footprint as well.

Sleeping Bag –I carried the Sierra Designs Zissou 23. The bag weighed 2 lb, 3 ounce in long. The EN comfort rating is 34 degrees for women and 23 for men. The bag used water resistant "Dri-Down" in its construction. I never "wet the bag" to test the capability, though on other trips it has stayed warm when damp from wet weather or condensation.

Pad – I used the Exped Hyperlite, medium version that weighs 12 ounces. Despite the light weight, the pad has a 3.3 R-value and a seemingly tough outer skin.

Cooking kit - GSI Outdoors Pinnacle Soloist Cookset. The pot, lid, cup and a foldable spoon weigh in at just under 10 ounces (leave the storage sack at home). My no name, folding canister stove fits inside the pot, and weighs 4 ounces. My stove cost less than ten bucks yet nothing, including the built-in igniter, ever failed. Google "cheap camping stove" and it should be at or near the top of the list. A small gas canister also fits in the pot, weighs 8 ounces full, and has lasted five days or more when heating water for instant oatmeal in the morning and a wholesome freeze-dried dinner at night.

Bear Canister – The Bearikade Weekender weighs in at 31 ounces and holds 650 cubic inches of chow. It is not cheap, but with carbon fiber construction it is lighter for its size than any other canister I found. Bearikades come in various sizes depending upon your needs.

Water Filter/Storage – Sawyer Mini Filter with a one-liter squeeze bag. I also used a small "bottled water" bottle to dip in the creeks to fill the squeeze bottle. Filtered water was kept in a one liter Nalgene bottle (the soft ones are lighter) and a one liter Gatorade bottle (lighter still). I also brought some chlorine dioxide tablets for back up. Everything together, except the actual water, weighed in at 12 ounces.

Small "essentials" – Petzl Tikka Plus headlamp weighed 4 oz including the AAA batteries. Small folding knife at 2 oz. Twenty five feet of rope at 3 oz. Pack rain cover at 4 oz. Small first aid kit at 4 oz which included a few Band-Aids, a gauze pad, tape, alcohol pads, anti-bacterial pads, sting relief pad, blister covers and a small anti-friction stick.

Smaller "essentials" – compass, mini camera tripod, small roll of duct tape, small container of insect repellent, 2 lighters, small multi-tool, small pepper spray (to irritate misbehaving bears or dogs…never used), sleeping pad repair kit (never used), sewing needle (never used) Everything together weighed around 8 oz.

Guide – The Tahoe Rim Trail Pocket Atlas weighed 2 oz.

Toiletries – Toilet paper, sanitizer, contact lens solution, case and mirror, toothbrush and paste, sunscreen, assorted pain relievers and other medications that might be needed, Wet Ones hand/face wipes. Total weight of 14 oz.

Clothing – REI nylon zip off pants/shorts, Outdoor Research lightweight t-shirt, short REI wool socks, nylon ball cap and Exofficio underwear. Spares in the pack were one pair of underwear, two pair of socks, light nylon pants, a 100 weight Columbia fleece pullover, another t-shirt, cheap rain pants, Outdoor Research packable rain jacket, an REI down vest, nylon gloves and watchman's cap. Crammed in Ziploc bags, the extra clothes weighed 3-3½ lbs. I never suffered from a lack of clothes, but at one time or another I did use every item of extra clothing.

Shoes - I used Saucony Xodus trail runners. The size 13 pair tipped the scales just over 2 lbs. In the pack was a 1lb, 1 oz pair of "camp/creek-crossing" sandals.

Electronics –The Spot Satellite Messenger weighed 5oz. I used it on a daily basis to let friend(s) and family know where I was and that I was OK. Luckily I never had to try the buttons that told them I was lost, had a shattered pelvis or lost a fight with a bear.
My iPhone with a waterproof case weighed 8 oz, and was used as a backup camera, GPS, Kindle book reader, journal, and as a phone with texts, email and internet when I had cell service.
My main camera was a Canon Powershot Elph 190 IS that weighed 5 oz. While it took some great shots, the pictures from the iPhone look, in many instances, as good or better.

There are ways to lower this weight, and many easy ways to increase it, but I felt like I had everything necessary to stay comfortable on the trail under normal circumstances.

Decision Time - Hopefully, this book has provided the information you need to decide whether or not to take the plunge and thru-hike the Tahoe Rim Trail. It truly is a great hike; epic yet achievable.

If you need more inspiration to commit to this adventure, look no further than the writings of John Muir, who spent significant time in the Sierra Nevada.

"Climb the mountains and get their good tidings. Nature's peace will flow into you as sunshine flows into trees. The winds will blow their own freshness into you, and the storms their energy, while cares will drop away from you like the leaves of Autumn."
John Muir, <u>The Mountains of California</u>

Made in the USA
Las Vegas, NV
21 February 2022

44330531R00028